Negative Thinking: How Negative Thoughts And Positive Thinking (Quick Start Guide)

Disclaimer

This eBook is for educational purposes only, and is not intended to be a substitute for professional counselling, therapy or medical treatment. Nothing in this eBook is intended to diagnose or treat any pathology or diseased condition of the mind or body. The author will not be held responsible for any results of reading or applying the information.

Table of Contents

About Colin G Smith

For over ten years now I have been driven to find the very best methods for creating effective personal change. If you are anything like me, you're probably interested in simple and straight-forward explanations. Practical stuff that gets results! I am a NLP Master Practitioner, writer & author who has written several books including:

- Difficult People: Dealing With Difficult People At Work
- EFT Tapping: How To Relieve Stress And Re-Energise Rapidly Using The Emotional Freedom Technique
- Neuro-Linguistic Programming NLP Techniques - Quick Start Guide

Visit My Amazon Author Page:

http://www.Amazon.com/Colin-G-Smith

Negative Verses Positive Thinking

Like it or not, we are what we think. Our thoughts define and refine our experience of life. Commonly used is the concept of seeing a glass half-full or half-empty to determine one's positive or negative outlook in life. Many self-help books and seminars are based around changing our thought patterns and have become commonplace in today's society.

Positive Thinking

This is the concept of facing challenges instead of avoiding them, looking for the best in others and focusing on one's abilities instead of weaknesses. Thinking positively helps determine the actions people take in a situation. Positive thinking also brings about the personal power needed to overcome stress.

Negative Thinking

This is whereby intrusive, involuntary and distorted thoughts plague the mind. Negative thoughts just pop up and dampen the spirit or overturn a light-hearted moment into a gloomy scenario. If given a chance, it is easy for this train of thought to become a habit and eventually lead to destructive behaviour. Giving in constantly to negative thinking makes it stronger and self-fulfilling.

Both Sides of the Coin

People that have developed a positive thinking mind-set tend to see problems as temporary and solvable. These thinkers give themselves a pat on the back for a job well done and, in team projects, share the guilt with others if there is a bad outcome. On the other hand, in negative thinking, people blame themselves when a failure occurs and never take the credit for their successful outcomes.

Pessimism is the easier route to take in comparison to optimism. It is much easier to let negative thoughts cloud the mind than to try and figure out how one can overcome problems. However, with effort, consistency and the right tools it is possible to reshape one's thinking patterns.

Positive thinking is healthy to both mind and body. Optimistic people are less stressed, have a greater resistance to common colds and other illnesses, tend to live longer, have more confidence and live happier lives. This is the exact opposite to negative thinking as it leads to mental health issues like depression and low self-esteem which affects one's life experience in the long run.

However, it is essential to note that optimism can also lead to underestimating the risks involved in a situation whereas pessimism can enable one to think more realistically and be cautious when making decisions.

The good news is that it is possible to overcome negative thinking by being grateful for the good things in life, surrounding yourself with optimistic people, helping someone else in need, involving yourself in enjoyable activities and never playing the victim in bad situations but instead choosing to take responsibility.

Getting The Blues Due To Negative Thinking Styles?

Constantly feeling moody, distressed and full of anxiety could be brought about by a number of things. What you need to know is that those depressive feelings are being brought about by negative thinking. When given a chance, negative thoughts can quickly turn into bad habits. Read on to identify the different unhelpful thinking styles; It might just help you in distance yourself from those negative thoughts and thus become more positive in those situations.

- Filtering is one style of faulty thinking. It involves only looking at the negative aspect of a situation and completely ignoring any positive and realistic aspects. Noticing only the bad stuff and magnifying it only makes the situation look more awful than it really is. Mental filtering is associated with the way we choose to remember things and can be a cause of depression.

- Emotional Reasoning is a situation whereby ones thoughts are solely based on what one might be feeling. A good example of this is someone that feels guilt and as a result of this believes that they must have done something wrong, even though they haven't.

- Catastrophizing situations is quite common. In this faulty thinking, people imagine that only the worst can happen. It is best described as, *"blowing things out of proportion."* Such negative thought patterns make people work themselves to a point that is beyond their control.

- Most people are slaves to labelling a specific quality into a global statement such as generalising that you are an idiot if you forget to buy something. In actuality this could lower one's self esteem affecting relationships with others.

- Polarised thinking is looking at things or people at the extreme with no room for in-between. With this type of faulty thinking, one is right or wrong, good or bad, with no middle ground for other conclusions. Thinking like this causes people to judge themselves and others too harshly.

- In everyday life, it is common to hear people say "*I should*" or "*I must.*" Constantly using these statements on ourselves and others makes us get angry when the rules are broken and eventually finding fault.

- Relating or personalising everything to ourselves is also a negative thinking style and in this instance, people compare themselves to others and use this to determine their worth.

Learning to identify negative thought patterns will assist you in overcoming unhelpful thinking styles and see the world in a more realistic way. This, however, does require a lot of discipline on our part but could be the best thing we can do for ourselves so as to lead better lives.

Depression And Negative Thinking

There are different types of negative thinking patterns that afflict different people in different ways. As you've learned some of these styles include; over generalisation, labelling and filtering. If left unchecked, the negative thoughts can easily lead to depression which will be much more damaging and difficult to deal with. In fact, in most cases, when the causes of depression are traced back, the root causes are negative or harmful thinking patterns.

One way in which negative thoughts develop into depression is through automation. In other words, we get so used to negative thoughts that they just pop up in our head every time we encounter a certain situation. For instance, if you sit in an exam and think, *"I am a failure,"* just because you failed in the last exam, this pattern may become automated and eventually you will drop your grades and depression sets in. When many negative thinking patterns are manifested in one person, the danger of depression is much greater.

Studies have shown that some negative thoughts are actually early warning signs of clinical depression. To ascertain this, a test known as the depression cognition scale, was developed. In the test, individuals are asked pre-defined questions regarding things like loneliness and hopelessness. They are then ranked on a scale ranging from strongly disagree to strongly agree. Modern psychology assesses the negative thinking patterns in a patient to diagnose depression and determine how extensive it is.

Due to the almost dismissible nature of small negative thoughts, millions of people suffer from clinical depression every year, something that could have been prevented. The best way of preventing an onset of depression is to surround yourself with close friends and positive-thinking people who will immediately notice any negative thinking and work to stem it off before it degenerates into depression.

You Become Who You Associate With: So Hang Out With Good

People!

If you do not have friends to help you, you can also do it yourself. Just remind yourself each time a negative thought pops into your head that it is not true. Just like negative thoughts can become automated and grow into depression, positive thoughts can also be automated and lead to something wonderful and satisfying. The more you think positive, the more you'll notice things changing for the better. You'll become more jovial, sociable, and your goals will become easier to attain. If, in any case, you realise that depression has already set in, it is time you sought professional help. Find a good therapist or life coach who can guide you out of negative thinking patterns and into positive thought patterns that will improve your entire life.

Gratitude and Optimism – The Two Vital Keys for Leading a Happier Life

Survival, safety and dealing with problems are the main focus points of life for most people trying to be happy and satisfied. There are pessimistic people who see failure before even trying and there are optimistic people who tend to see the bright side in every problem. There are people who are always grateful with their past and present, and there are also those who are ungrateful and never stop complaining. If you want to lead a happier life, you can improve your experience by practicing gratitude and optimism.

Gratitude is the expression of being thankful for everything you have come across at present or might experience in the future. It is a feeling of appreciation that blossoms your soul and mind. You can value your past and realise your worth by being grateful for whatever good or bad (learning experience) has happened so far.

Optimism is the powerful ability of seeing an opportunity in every difficulty. An optimistic person imagines brighter days even in the hours of darkness and misery. This state of mind helps you in looking forward positively toward the things you might be expecting or not.

There are many benefits to gratitude. For example, a grateful person does not feel depressed and faces all stressful situations with faith in a positive outcome. Gratitude helps you express positive emotions toward every happening. You'll feel more satisfied with your life and become optimistic. You'll praise your mind and body, and thus your creative abilities will start blossoming.

Similarly, the main advantages of optimism include resilience and persistence in dealing with life's challenges. An optimistic person has better mental and emotional health. He becomes more confident and achieves his life goals successfully. The pleasures and joys of life are more visible and enjoyable for optimistic people. Optimism keeps you healthier by being able to effectively deal with stressful situations.

Gratitude and optimism go hand in hand. Being an optimistic person, you'll be grateful with whatever happens in your life. You'll appreciate your personal life, family, professional life, income, goals and accomplishments. You'll see things from a different perspective than a pessimistic person. You'll face life's challenges by utilising your creative problem-solving abilities.

In a nutshell, gratitude and optimism lead to a happier, healthier, and successful life. So start practicing being grateful and optimistic and look for success where others might see failure. Look for ways which can make your life better and brighter!

"Optimism is the faith that leads to achievement. Nothing can be done without hope and confidence." - Helen Keller

"Everything can be taken from a man but one thing: the last of human freedoms - to choose one's attitude in any given set of circumstances, to choose one's own way." - Viktor E. Frankl

"The capacity for hope is the most significant fact of life. It provides human beings with a sense of destination and the energy to get started." - Norman Cousins

How To Develop The Habit Of Gratitude & Optimism

It's a really good idea to develop the habit of having a grateful and optimistic outlook to life because it's a direct antidote to stress and negative thinking. The good news is it may be easier than you think to gain a healthy positive mind-set.

Here's a simple way you can do it:

- Buy a new diary or journal

- Every evening before your go to bed write down twenty things you are grateful for. This could be obvious things like having a loving family to really simple things that you appreciate such as the little sparrows you see on your fence.

- Allow yourself to feel your heart open up or soften as you think of these things. Really feel it.

- Ask, *"What three things can I look forward to tomorrow?"* This could be simple things such as a cup of fresh coffee etc.

- Repeat this every day so it becomes a ritual. Mark in your diary to check how your experience of life has changed using this simple task 21 days from now.

Polarised Thinking In A Dual Universe

The Universe we find ourselves in is dualistic in nature. Everything has it's own complimentary opposite. We have the positive and the negative. There is light within darkness. That is what the ancient and profound Taoist symbol of Yin and Yang represents.

The Taoist Farmer's Story

There was a Chinese farmer.

One day his horse ran away.

All his neighbours exclaimed how terrible this was, but the farmer simply said, "Maybe."

A few days later the horse returned and brought two wild horses with it.

The neighbours all rejoiced at his good fortune, but the farmer just said, "Maybe."

The next day the farmer's son tried to ride one of the wild horses; the horse threw him and broke his leg.

The neighbours all offered their sympathy for his misfortune, but the farmer again said, "Maybe."

The next week conscription officers came to the village to take young men for the army.

They rejected the farmer's son because of his broken leg.

When the neighbours told him how lucky he was, the farmer replied, "Maybe."

Of course the story could go on and on... The point that's being made is that your experience of *reality* depends upon your point of view. We choose whether to view something as positive or negative. Every experience in life has positive and negative aspects to it. With our mind or consciousness we direct our attention.

Serbian Author and Mystic, Zivorad Slavinski, has developed many spiritual growth systems, over several decades, based on the dualistic nature of reality or put more simply; Polarities. Here is an excerpt from his book, * *"Return to Oneness"* that explains the human condition caught up in polarities:

"When two polar forces inside an individual are in strong conflict, they often make a neurotic structure. Then we define one component of such an experience as good, the other as bad, we identify with the good one and fight against the bad."

"The dualistic nature of this universe sets the stage for many splits in our mind, as well as for many neuroses which are the most frequent disturbances of our time. Dichotomies like I and Others, We and They, Good and Bad, Light and Darkness...constantly draw us into one or the other side of such a split."

"To transcend such states of inner breaks, wise men, shamans and practitioners of spiritual practice created and applied, since ancient times, techniques of uniting opposites into higher synthesises of wholeness."

"Such practical knowledge does not come easily. Only through permanent use and application can practitioners advance on the path of integration and self-realisation. Every moment is a test because dual forces tempt us permanently, trying to pull us into themselves, into separation and suffering."

"For our practical life this is important: In every pair of polarities that manifest inside us we estimate the dominate polarity as less valuable. The moment opposing forces enter reconciliation, when they unite into one, all conflicts, awkwardness and neurosis coming out of them vanish."

"We feel this world from the stage of dualities, because we learned from early childhood to experience it that way. We have a strong tendency to experience some people as good or bad, some situation as favourable or unfavourable, a point of view as right or wrong, self and others as valuable or worthless."

"The world we live in is built on duality, as an arena of opposites inside, which most of us live our life through. In the universe of matter, energy, time and space (MEST) it is not possible to find one

16

phenomenon or state, without their opposites being there. Light does not exist without darkness, warm without cold, good without the idea of bad, happiness without suffering. The old proverb says that not one picture is painted just with light, there must be shadows on it as well." (Pg.5 Return To Oneness)

* Zivorad Mihajlovic Slavinski. Return to Oneness: Principles and Practice of Spiritual Technology. 2009.

The End of Words

It's well known that getting stuff out of your head onto paper helps you de-stress and gain some respite from negative self talk. Simply writing your thoughts out onto paper can be a beneficial exercise. However there is a superior method that makes use of the dualistic nature of our problems and it enables us to empty the heavy problem content from our mind faster. Using the example of *difficult relationship* we could say, *"it is painful,"* on the negative polarity, and on the positive polarity we could say, *"it helps me learn patience."*

The following *End of Words* exercise is very simple. It's one of those techniques that is simple yet profound. It was devised by Zivorad Slavinski's daughter Ivana, inspired by his teachings over the years. The most important aspect is that it makes use of the *Alternating Technique* which Slavinski discovered after many years of doing change-work. It really speeds things up!

Here in his own words is how he discovered this phenomena:

"Some people know the story of my discovery of the Alternating Technique. For those who don't, I will go through it very shortly. All recent years I kept in my mind the statement of our living in dual universe. And couple of years ago I had a funny experience. Passing by a garden in the outskirts of Belgrade I noticed two men trying to pull down a large wooden pillar. Its lower part was buried deeply in the ground. They swung it left and right, forward and backward and in about 5 minutes pulled it down. A question popped up in my mind: 'How long would they need if they had tried to do it by pushing the pillar in only one direction? Much, much more. Hours or maybe days.'"

"In that moment I had a valuable cognition and the whole idea of the new, more efficient Alternating Technique. I went home, called my family members and some friends and the next day I created a new kind of Intensive. I was right. The new Alternating Technique was extremely fast." (Pg.137 Return To Oneness)

The End Of Words Technique

With the following method you can write out your short answers, allow a trusted friend to listen to your answers or just use a text editor on your computer. You may be surprised how quickly you can empty your mind of *junk* and find a sense of inner peace...

1. What is the problem you want to solve specifically?

State this as your subjective experience. e.g.) *"I'm not earning enough money,"* more specifically becomes, *"I don't feel I am capable of earning a decent living."*

You now alternate between the following two questions and write down what comes to mind. Keep going until you've no words left; The End of Words. It will come sooner than you might think!

- What's bad about the problem?

- What's good about the problem?

2. At the **End of Words** ask yourself, *"What is the matter with the problem we started from?"*

"Do you still feel it as a problem?"

The Power Of Accepting Reality

A lot of the negative feelings we experience are caused by distorted thinking. However, of course, there are unpleasant things that happen in the real world and we have to deal with them. Quite often though we try to push problems away in the hope that they will disappear. The Buddha repeated a great maxim to his followers:

"You Become What You Resist"

In *Return to Oneness* Slavinski writes; *"If a man does not understand the laws of the dual universe, he has the tendency to resist and confront negative polarities and the experiences which follow them. The resistance to any negative experience means we are trying to make it weaker, and such resistance just make it stronger and more persisting. Resistance causes persistence! The resistance is the investing of energy to prevent some manifestation, in other words, to stop it, change it or destroy it. When you invest energy to stop, change or destroy some manifestation, you invest energy in it, and therefore make it stronger and more real."* (Pg.9 Return To Oneness)

What is Reality Anyway?

Our experience of reality is created by the data coming in through the senses. We see, hear and feel things and our mind generates multiple thoughts about all phenomena. This process happens very quickly, and beyond our conscious awareness. Our memories are made up of images and sounds and our thoughts and feelings get attached to them.

The 4 Elements Of Experience

All of our experiences are a combination of the following four elements:

1. Image or Picture

Part of our experience is stored as internal imagery. e.g.) A scene of a beautiful sunset.

2. Emotion

We have various emotions good and bad. e.g.) Contentment

3. Body Sensation

Our feelings are generated by different body sensations. e.g.) A slow energy rolling forward from the heart to the hands.

4. Thought

Our thoughts are infinite. We can have abstract and logical thoughts on many different levels. e.g.) This is wonderful!

So with this knowledge we can begin to understand that if we can confront these four elements of an experience we can learn to accept the reality of it rather than resisting and persisting the problem. And even better, we can use this know-how to create some rather powerful process's of change.

Verbal Reduction & Expansion (VRE)

What you are about to discover is an amazing process that incorporates the reality of polarities and the four elements of experience in a way that enables you to transform your problems quickly and easily. Again this is another original technique created by Zivorad M. Slavinski. In his own words this is how he came upon this wonderful process;

"Data, which I have been collecting for a long time, cumulated some energy and in one moment there happened a quantum jump as with an electrical spark and a new revelation appeared. I was strongly impressed by the thought that nations, which lost their language, vanished from existence.

It brought me to the creation of the method of Verbal Reduction and Expansion (VRE). Its basic idea was my own discovery that with the reduction and vanishing of the words with which we describe a problem that problem simultaneously vanishes." (Pg. 315 Return To Oneness)

The process works by getting you to accept and experience all elements of a problem you have and then reduces your linguistic representation of that problem step by step until it disappears! This is a fascinating technique that you'll better understand once you've read through the following example and tried it out for yourself...

Example of Verbal Reduction & Expansion (VRE)

The Problem:

I feel stressed out about my lack of money.

Reduction:

"Describe to me your *present* state (or situation), how you feel about the situation, in **FOUR** short, concise sentences. Write these sentences down."

Money stresses me out. The lack of money causes me to feel stressed! I wish it was easier to make more money. I need to make more money.

Image: Me digging a trench
Emotion: Drudgery
Body Sensation: Sinking feeling
Thought: Man does this get easier?!

"Describe to me your *present* state (or situation), how you feel about the situation, in **THREE** short, concise sentences. Write these sentences down."

I wish I could easily make more money! It would be good to double my income within a month! How difficult can it be?!

Image: Me pondering
Emotion: Curiosity
Body Sensation: Energy in hands
Thought: hmmm, maybe it's possible

"Describe to me your *present* state (or situation), how you feel about the situation, in **TWO** short, concise sentences. Write these sentences down."

I want to make more money. I'm wondering if it's possible to do it quickly within say a month or two.

Image: Me testing plans out on paper.
Emotion: Possibility
Body Sensation: Heart opening
Thought: Maybe it is possible!

"Describe to me your _present_ state (or situation), how you feel about the situation, in **ONE** short, concise sentences. Write these sentences down."

I want to make more money.

Image: Me counting cash
Emotion: Feeling good
Body Sensation: Heart
Thought: This provides me with more possibilities!

"Now tell me how you feel in only **ONE WORD** or one concept. Write this word or concept down."

Possibility!

Image: Sunrise horizon
Emotion: Joy
Body Sensation: Heart opening
Thought: The future's full of possibilities!

In the example above the problem disappeared within the Verbal Reduction Phase. There was no need to go into the Verbal Expansion Phase. As you will find out when you play with this yourself, the _miracle_ can often happen in just the Reduction phase! Pick a problem you've got and give this method a go now. The steps are below and you can do this on paper or with your computer's text editor. Remember you're done when all the elements are positive – _there's no need to carry on once you've reached that positive state._

The Verbal Reduction & Expansion (VRE) Technique

Elicit the specific problem (emotional state.)

Reduction:

"Describe to me your *present* state (or situation), how you feel about the situation, in **FOUR** short, concise sentences. Write these sentences down."

Image:
Emotion:
Body Sensation:
Thought:

"Describe to me your *present* state (or situation), how you feel about the situation, in **THREE** short, concise sentences. Write these sentences down."

Image:
Emotion:
Body Sensation:
Thought:

"Describe to me your *present* state (or situation), how you feel about the situation, in **TWO** short, concise sentences. Write these sentences down."

Image:
Emotion:

Body Sensation:
Thought:

"Describe to me your _present_ state (or situation), how you feel about the situation, in **ONE** short, concise sentences. Write these sentences down."

Image:
Emotion:
Body Sensation:
Thought:

"Now tell me how you feel in only **ONE WORD** or one concept. Write this word or concept down."

Image:
Emotion:
Body Sensation:
Thought:

Expansion:

"How do you feel about your situation now? Tell me how you feel in **ONE** sentence. Write this sentence down."

Image:
Emotion:
Body Sensation:
Thought:

"How do you feel about your situation now? Tell me how you feel in **TWO** sentences. Write these sentences down."

Image:
Emotion:
Body Sensation:
Thought:

"How do you feel about your situation now? Tell me how you feel in **THREE** sentences. Write these sentences down."

Image:
Emotion:
Body Sensation:
Thought:

"How do you feel about your situation now? Tell me how you feel in **FOUR** sentences. Write these sentences down."

Image:
Emotion:
Body Sensation:
Thought:

"How do you feel about your situation now?

Expanding Positivity Into All Possible Futures

When you've *disappeared the problem* and attained a nice positive state it can be a good idea to stabilise this state and expand it into your future(s). It's actually quite straight forward:

1. Notice the good feelings. Feel those positive feelings as strongly as possible.

2. Now imagine sending that positive energy way off in front of you, out into the Universe.

3. Now imagine sending that positive energy way off in behind you, out into the Universe.

4. Now imagine sending that positive energy way off to the left of you, out into the Universe.

5. Now imagine sending that positive energy way off to the right of you, out into the Universe.

6. Now imagine sending that positive energy way off above you, out into the Universe.

7. Now imagine sending that positive energy way off below you, out into the Universe.

Personal Development: Taking Responsibility

Taking charge of your own personal development is a big responsibility for anyone. It's not something that you can do overnight. Most of us make mistakes when it comes to our own self growth. Sometimes we think that improving ourself is all about looking at the success of other people and applying the same principles to ourself. This is one of the most critical mistakes of self improvement because it is not who you really are. Personal development is about yourself and your goals in life, including the things that you'll have to change if you want to achieve your goals.

If you want to overcome negative thinking and improve your life, a good start is to write down some new goals that _excite_ you! You need to have an idea about what you really want to get out of life before you can start worthwhile self improvement. Take your time thinking about your goals. Choose your goals carefully and use them as a basis for continuous self improvement.

There will be times when you start doubting your own capabilities. When this happens it's an opportunity to use the tools you've learned in this book. Transform any negative thoughts that appear, accelerate your self-growth and get closer to achieving the goals that inspire you.

The quality of your life is always up to you. There are many different tips and advice about self-development that you can consider, but all of them are only guidelines. Taking responsibility for your own personal development is the best thing that you can do if you want to be happy and successful in life.

Printed in Great Britain
by Amazon

24986711R00020